OUR GOD IS
A BLESSING GOD

DAMIAN KYLE

CALVARY CHAPEL PUBLISHING

SANTA ANA, CALIFORNIA

Published by Calvary Chapel Publishing (CCP),
a resource ministry of Calvary Chapel of Costa Mesa
3800 South Fairview Road
Santa Ana, CA 92704

First printing, 2002

All Scripture quotations in this book, unless otherwise indicated, are taken from the New King James Version. Copyright © 1982, Thomas Nelson, Inc. Used by permission. All rights reserved.

Scripture quotations marked (KJV) are taken from the King James Version of the Bible.

ISBN 1-931667-60-8

Printed in the United States of America.

Cover Illustration by: Lary Stucker

PREFACE

Who is God, and what is He truly like?

These are two of the most important questions any of us will address in life. Finding the answers to these questions is not always easy because it seems almost everyone has their own ideas and theories, many of them contradictory. And with so many voices, opinions, and so-called experts, one can almost give up hope of ever finding answers. Fortunately, God rises up from the pages of Scripture to answer the questions Himself, and the answers are better than any of us could have hoped or imagined!

...Who is so great a God as our God?

Psalm 77:13

God's blessings,

Damian Kyle

DEDICATION

Dedicated to my wife, Karin.

And the LORD spoke to Moses, saying:

> *"Speak to Aaron and his sons, saying,*
>
> > *'This is the way you shall bless the children of Israel. Say to them:*
> >
> > > *"The LORD bless you and keep you;*
> > >
> > > *The LORD make His face shine upon you,*
> > >
> > > *And be gracious to you;*
> > >
> > > *The LORD lift up His countenance upon you,*
> > >
> > > *And give you peace."'*
> >
> *So they shall put My name on the children of Israel, and I will bless them."*

Numbers 6:22-27

OUR GOD'S HEART

The Book of Numbers was written to a wandering people—to God's people. In a very real sense, everything He writes to His people in the entire volume of the Book, He writes to a wandering people—a people who are not at home in this fallen world, a people who are strangers and pilgrims anywhere you find them, strangers and pilgrims until you find them home in Heaven's glory.

1

OUR GOD IS A BLESSING GOD

Because the Lord knows this to be the condition of His people, He knows that we are a people in need of special blessing. In this world, the believer in the Lord Jesus faces all of the things that everyone else faces. We face the threat of crime, the threat of violence, and the threat of war. We face the threat of job loss, the threat of economic instability, and the threat of financial hardship. We face the threat of debilitating illnesses and diseases. We face threats against our families, difficulties in relationships and marriages, and all the challenges and demands involved in raising children. If a Christian man is a farmer, he must face the same challenges that weather presents to believing and unbelieving farmers alike. If he is a believing rancher, he must face the same herd-threatening diseases that an unbelieving rancher faces.

These are the words that God wanted His people to have ringing in their ears and in their hearts....

In addition to all of these things, however, the child of God also faces things unique to believers in Christ. We face persecution, isolation, and rejection as a result of our faith in Jesus, even in some of the most cherished and intimate relationships in our lives. We face reviling, mocking, and scorning for our beliefs. We face a very real and unceasing spiritual warfare that the world knows nothing about. We face constant temptations to sin and constant pressure to compromise God's Word and live on the same level as the world around us. We uniquely face the challenge of raising godly children equipped to go against the stream of this world. The list goes on and on.

Thus, with so much working against us in this very fallen world, the Lord knows that we are in need of supernatural power and strength, and He has given them to us in the Person of the Holy Spirit. God knows that we are in need of supernatural wisdom and truth, and He has given them to us in His Word. But He also knows that as His people we are in need of supernatural encouragement. In this passage, we have the Lord Himself telling Moses to instruct the priests regarding the blessing that He wanted to have regularly pronounced over His people. This blessing was to be pronounced over the children of Israel at the conclusion of the spiritual gatherings of His people.

In other words, these are the words that God wanted His people to have ringing in their ears and in their hearts when they left any assembly associated with Him. At that time in Jewish history, the people met at the tabernacle at least once a day for the morning service and sacrifice; and on special days, they would meet there multiple times in a single day. Therefore, they would hear this benediction at least once a day. It almost seems as if God was thinking, "I want them to hear this so often that they know it frontward, backward, and sideways. I want it etched into the deepest parts of their hearts and minds."

In this blessing is the reassurance of six truths concerning the Lord, six things that the Lord wants us, as His people, to be continually reminded of concerning Himself. He knows that with so much working against us in this world as His people that we need a daily reassurance of His heart toward us to maintain a proper perspective.

OUR GOD IS A BLESSING GOD

The first truth that He wanted declared over His people was, "The LORD bless you." God wants His people to be continually reassured that He is a God who blesses. On a daily basis, He wants this truth planted in our ears, in our minds, and in our hearts—the God we serve is a blessing God. This truth reassures us that He is aware of our needs, and He will provide for them. The Lord knows that we have daily needs, and He knows that we need a daily reminder that He is going to provide for our needs in this life.

Our Lord wants us continually reassured that though the path we are on is not the easiest path to walk in this life, it is the path of blessing—His blessing. Why? Because our God is a blessing God. He is eager to bless us, He loves to bless us, and He will bless us. The Lord wants every single one of His children to possess a sanctified boldness and confidence in Him that He is a blessing God.

The Apostle Paul certainly had this great confidence in God as a blessing God. He put it this way, "What then shall we say to these things? If God is for us, who can be against us? He who did not spare His own Son, but delivered Him up for us all, how shall He not with Him also freely give us all things?" (Romans 8:31-32)

OUR GOD IS A BLESSING GOD

Jesus declared in the Sermon on the Mount,

> Therefore I say to you, *do not worry about your life, what you will eat or what you will drink; nor about your body, what you will put on.* Is not life more than food and the body more than clothing? Look at the birds of the air, for they neither sow nor reap nor gather into barns; yet your heavenly Father feeds them. Are you not of more value than they? Which of you by worrying can add one cubit to his stature?
>
> So why do you worry about clothing? Consider the lilies of the field, how they grow: they neither toil nor spin; and yet I say to you that even Solomon in all his glory was not arrayed like one of these. Now if God so clothes the grass of the field, which today is, and tomorrow is thrown into the oven, *will He not much more clothe you, O you of little faith?*
>
> Therefore do not worry, saying, "What shall we eat?" or "What shall we drink?" or "What shall we wear?" For after all these things the Gentiles seek. *For your heavenly Father knows that you need all these things.* But seek first the kingdom of God and His righteousness, *and all these things shall be added to you.*

> Matthew 6:25-33, emphasis mine

Just because the so-called "health and wealth" or "prosperity" teaching has taken things far beyond the teaching of the Bible, that doesn't mean we are to overreact in the other direction and neglect the great confidence in our Lord as a blessing and a providing God. David said in Psalm 37, "I have been young, and now am old; yet I have not seen the righteous forsaken, nor his descendants begging bread" (v. 25).

Like David, I too have been young, and though I am not yet old, I am getting older. My wife and I have two grown daughters, and awhile back I was thinking about some of the lessons I have learned the hard way over the years in my walk with the Lord and what I would tell younger people like them so that they could avoid some of the pitfalls that I fell into. One of the things that I would warn anyone

> *Every moment I have spent in my Christian life in "anxious thought" or worry has been a complete waste of time.*

against would be wasting even a moment of time in what the Bible refers to as "anxious thought," or worry. Every moment I have spent in my Christian life in "anxious thought" or worry has been a complete waste of time. I bear witness that in every situation in my life, the Lord has proven Himself over and over again to be a blessing God. He has never failed to be that in my life. That isn't to say that He has always done things the way that I have wanted Him to, but He has always done what was best, and time bore it out. I have found that when He has said "No" to one thing in my life, it has always been to do something better.

I would say to all, but especially to those who are younger, do not waste even a moment's time in anxious thought. Much better to stop and cry out, "Lord, this anxious thought isn't worthy of You because I know

OUR GOD IS A BLESSING GOD

You are a blessing God." Perhaps today, we need to speak to our downcast souls as David did, "Why art thou cast down, O my soul? and why art thou disquieted in me? Hope thou in God: for I shall yet praise him for the help of his countenance" (Psalm 42:5, KJV). Our God is a blessing God. Perhaps, however, some of us have ceased to live in a daily expectation of His blessing, where we wake up in the morning with the anticipation that God is going to bless us today.

Perhaps there was a time in your Christian walk when you woke up with that expectation. However, as time has passed and you have become more "mature" as a Christian, you have lost that sanctified boldness in God as a blessing God. Now you go long days, weeks, months, and years with no expectation that God is going to bless you today. I want to remind you that our Lord is a blessing God. Perhaps now would be a good time to take a moment to repeat to yourself a few times, "My God is a blessing God, my God is a blessing God," until the Holy Spirit blows upon you as a "smoking flax" and brings that expectation of God's blessing to a full and God-honoring flame once again.

Our God is a blessing God.

OUR GOD IS A KEEPING GOD

The second truth that He wanted declared over His people was, "The LORD...keep thee" (KJV). Our Lord wants us to be constantly reassured that our God is a keeping God. How we need this reassurance in such an evil and uncertain world!

The Psalmist wrote of this declaring,

> I will lift up my eyes to the hills — from whence comes my help? My help comes from the LORD, Who made heaven and earth.

> He will not allow your foot to be moved; He who *keeps* you will not slumber. Behold, He who keeps Israel shall neither slumber nor sleep.

> The LORD is your *keeper*; the LORD is your shade at your right hand. The sun shall not strike you by day, nor the moon by night.

OUR GOD IS A BLESSING GOD

The LORD *shall preserve* you from all evil; He *shall preserve* your soul. The LORD *shall preserve* your going out and your coming in from this time forth, and even forevermore.

Psalm 121, emphasis mine

The Hebrew word used in this blessing means, "to keep, to watch, to guard, to hedge about." In ancient times, a city that had a wall around it had a tremendous advantage if they were attacked. That is why homes within the walls were much more expensive than the ones outside of the walls.

He will keep us spiritually no matter how great the spiritual warfare from without or how overwhelming the crushing fears from within.

Protection has always been, and is still considered, a desirable and valuable asset in this fallen world. Here God is declaring Himself to be a living, divine wall or hedge of protection around our individual lives. That is the ultimate protection. That protection allows us as His people to be at rest while living in a very dangerous world.

This knowledge gives us the reassurance that He will keep us spiritually no matter how great the spiritual warfare from without or how overwhelming the crushing fears from within (2 Corinthians 7:5). Jesus declared much the same thing in John 17, as He prayed to the Father, "Now I am no longer in the world, but these are in the world, and I come to You. Holy Father, *keep* through Your name those whom You have given Me, that they may be one as We are. While I was with them in the world, I *kept* them in Your name" (vs. 11-12a, emphasis mine). From the time that we believed in the Lord Jesus for our salvation to the time that we go to be with Him, He is not going to lose a single one of us. He is going to be faithful to keep every one that is His.

That our God keeps us is also a daily reassurance that He will protect us physically. We need to have that assurance today, don't we? We live in an evil and violent world. It seems that every time we read the newspaper or watch television, we are exposed to another torrent of bad news that can strike fear in the strongest of hearts. When I was a young boy, armed robberies and car thefts were very rare, and kidnappings and mass murders were almost nonexistent. Today, they have become commonplace. I remember when I was in elementary school hearing of a mass murder in the San Francisco Bay area. In that day, it was so shocking that my parents hid the newspaper from us children for several days so that we would not be exposed to it. But today such things, and worse, have become our daily portion.

Jesus declared that such social, moral, national, and international instability, including widespread religious persecution, would mark the world in what the Bible refers to as "the latter times" or the Last Days, and that these things would grow in intensity and frequency like the contractions of a woman giving birth. But in the midst of it, "God is our refuge and strength, a very *present help* in trouble. Therefore we will not fear, even though the earth be removed, and though the mountains be carried into the midst of the sea" (Psalm 46:1-2, emphasis mine). The Psalmist concludes by declaring, "Be still and know that I am God; I will be exalted among the nations, I will be exalted in the earth! The LORD of hosts is with us. The God of Jacob is our refuge" (Psalm 46:10-11).

He is every bit our keeper when He allows difficulty and then keeps us through that difficulty to the other side.

When we think of our God as a keeping God, there is a tendency to think of His "keeping" one-dimensionally, that is, if He is a keeping God, it will always be demonstrated in His keeping us from trial and difficulty. Then, when something difficult occurs in our lives, we incorrectly conclude that God has somehow failed in His promise to keep us. However, when God speaks of "keeping," the word also carries the idea of "through." He is every bit our keeper when He allows difficulty and then keeps us through that difficulty to the other side.

I think of the children of Israel as Moses was leading them out of Egypt. When they came to that place where they had the Red Sea before them and Pharaoh's chariots fast approaching behind them, that was a very difficult trial—crushingly difficult. In fact, they literally feared for their lives. We are told that as Pharaoh and his chariot-equipped army drew near, the children of Israel lifted up their eyes, and seeing them, they were very afraid and began to cry out to God. They also cried out to Moses, "Because there were no graves in Egypt, have you taken us away to die in the wilderness?" (Exodus 14:11) But God delivered them by parting the Red Sea, keeping them through the trial rather than from it. To be kept from that trial rather than through it would have robbed them of an experience of God's power in their lives, an experience that they would glory in for all of their lives and history.

So it is with us. How little we would know of God's power and how weak would be our faith and godly character if God only kept us from difficulty rather than also being a God who keeps us through difficulty.

I think of David in all of this. Consider how much God allowed him to go through to prepare him to be the king of Israel. Late in life, as David penned Psalm 23, he declared, "Yea, though I walk through the valley of the shadow of death, I will fear no evil; *for You are with me*" (v. 4, emphasis mine). It was in going through even life-threatening difficulties that David learned things about the presence of God that he might not have learned if he had been kept from trial.

Shadrach, Meshach, and Abed-nego, the three young Hebrew men who served with Daniel in Babylon, refused to bow down to Nebuchadnezzar's golden image. As a result, they were thrown into the fiery furnace. But in the midst of that fire, the Lord Himself walked with them. God did not keep them from the fiery trial, but He kept them through the fiery trial. It was in the furnace that they experienced a communion with the Lord that they might not have otherwise known.

Sometimes when we make an uncompromising stand for the Lord in our workplace or elsewhere, we might think that God will reward us by keeping us from difficult consequences. Oftentimes, He will instead allow a fire to burn around us, but in the midst of it, He will make His presence known in special ways and will never allow the fire or trial to harm us. The only thing that was burned by the fire was the rope that bound them. Very often, the Lord will take us through difficulty in order to burn away and loose us from things that would otherwise keep us bound, things like the fear of man or the opinions of other people.

I think of Noah who was not kept from the flood, but through it. The prophet Daniel was not kept from the lion's den, but through it. Jeremiah the prophet was not kept from having to watch the death of a nation, but through it. The Apostle Paul knew much of this. He was not kept from the stoning at Lystra, but through it (Acts 14:8-20). He wrote to the church at Corinth:

> Blessed be the God and Father of our Lord Jesus Christ, the Father of mercies and God of all comfort, *who comforts us in all our tribulation, that we may be able to comfort those who are in any trouble, with the comfort with which we ourselves are comforted by God.* For as the sufferings of Christ abound in us, so our consolation also abounds through Christ. Now if we are afflicted, it is for your consolation and salvation, which is effective for enduring the same sufferings which we also suffer. Or if we are comforted, it is for your consolation and salvation. And our hope for you is steadfast, because we know that as you are partakers of the sufferings, so also you will partake of the consolation.

OUR GOD IS A KEEPING GOD

For we do not want you to be ignorant, brethren, of our trouble which came to us in Asia: *that we were burdened beyond measure, above strength, so that we despaired even of life. Yes, we had the sentence of death in ourselves, that we should not trust in ourselves but in God who raises the dead, who delivered us from so great a death, and does deliver us; in whom we trust that He will still deliver us.*

2 Corinthians 1:3-10, emphasis mine

He is testifying to the fact that God is a keeping God, but that while He is able to keep us from difficulty, when He chooses to keep us through difficulty, it is in order that we might learn things we might not otherwise learn. In this particular chapter in Paul's life, it was in order that he might come to know God as the "God of all comfort" and to learn in a greater measure not to trust in himself but in God. These were valuable lessons indeed.

When He chooses to keep us through difficulty, it is in order that we might learn things we might not otherwise learn.

Even death does not mean that God has failed in His promise to keep us. Barring the Rapture, just as with the apostles, there will come a time for us to go home to Heaven, but that will only occur when God's purposes for our lives here are over. The death of a saint does not mean that God has failed or ceased in His promise to keep us. Instead, it is then that we discover His commitment to keep us does not stop with this life but continues until He has kept us right into the glory of Heaven.

15

OUR GOD IS A BLESSING GOD

I have always been comforted by the Bible's account of God's two witnesses in Revelation chapter 11. In this passage, judging by the miracles they perform, it would appear that one of the witnesses is Elijah and the other is Moses. Regardless of their identities, it is interesting to note that no attempt to harm them is successful until they finish their testimonies or their ministries for the Lord.

> And I will give power to *my two witnesses*, and they will prophesy one thousand two hundred and sixty days, clothed in sackcloth.
>
> These are the two olive trees and the two lampstands standing before the God of the earth.
>
> *And if anyone wants to harm them*, fire proceeds from their mouth and devours their enemies. *And if anyone wants to harm them*, he must be killed in this manner.
>
> These have power to shut heaven, so that no rain falls in the days of their prophecy; and they have power over waters to turn them to blood, and to strike the earth with all plagues, as often as they desire.
>
> *When they finish their testimony*, the beast that ascends out of the bottomless pit will make war against them, overcome them, and kill them.
>
> Revelation 11:3-7, emphasis mine

OUR GOD IS A KEEPING GOD

I believe that as we live a life of simple obedience to Him, our lives are supernaturally protected until our ministries are finished, and then, there being no further reason to remain separated from seeing Him face to face, God takes us home to Heaven.

Until I came to know the Lord, I had, if not a fear of death, a deep concern about it. I was quite conscious of its reality. I ate bran, raw, by the tablespoon twenty years before bran became the health food buzzword it is today. I ran twenty-five miles a week after work and drank all kinds of healthy concoctions (all of which is fine), but I was doing it out of a fear of death, very conscious of my own mortality. Now I rest, knowing that the number of my days are in His hands, that my life will not be one day longer or shorter than He intends. I rest in the knowledge that my God is a keeping God who will be absolutely faithful not only to keep me through this life until my work is done, but then keep me right into the everlasting life to come.

Our heavenly Father knows that His people can have very legitimate concerns about their physical and spiritual safety in this world. Thus He gives us a daily reminder that He is a keeping God — a God who watches out for us, guards us, puts a hedge around us so that we might live every day free from fears for our safety and from the very real bondage of the fear of death (Hebrews 2:15).

Our God is a blessing God. *Our God is a keeping God.*

The LORD make His face shine upon you....

OUR GOD IS A SMILING GOD

Notice thirdly, in verse 25, "The LORD make His face shine upon you." The Lord wants us to be daily reminded of the fact that when He looks at us, He smiles. That is what this passage means. A shining face is a smiling face. The image is of Him smiling, of His face beaming towards me. A smiling face is also the face of someone who is pleased. It's the face of someone who is enjoying themselves and the company that they're in.

It is a grandpa's face.

I know. You see, I'm an authority concerning all of this because I am a grandpa, or poppa as I am called; and believe me when I tell you that the face that is described here is a grandparent's face. Something funny happens to you when you become a grandparent. Before you become a grandparent, you see these license plate holders that say, "Ask me about my grandchildren." As I have seen them through the years, I've thought to myself "Yeah right, like I'm going to ask you about your grandchildren! Don't people have any shame? These people are out of control!"

Then I had grandchildren, and my attitude changed completely. What you become as a grandparent is like a sickness, a virus. Don't get angry at these people who have bumper stickers, license plate holders, and stacks of pictures of their grandchildren always within reach. They are to be pitied because they're incurable, and it can't be helped.

I have the blessing and privilege of seeing my grandchildren regularly because we live in the same town. When I walk into the front door of my house and my grandchildren are there, I don't care who else is in the house. I don't notice them. My face just beams, and all sense of dignity goes at the very sight of them. When they were babies, sometimes they would be with me in my office at the church, and I would rock them while singing some silly song, making faces and doing things that are so undignified. But as a grandparent, you don't care who hears or sees, and you don't care what anyone else thinks. Your face is shining with pleasure toward them. You love them and enjoy their company beyond description. A shining face is a grandpa's face.

God's face shines with pleasure toward us as His people.

God's face shines with pleasure toward us as His people. He isn't angry with us, and He isn't disappointed in us. He isn't a God who is by nature grumpy and unhappy with us until we do something nice to change His mind and change His mood. He loves us, and He loves us so much that the very thought of us, the very sight of us, puts a beaming smile on His face! He isn't the kind of God who can't be pleased. Those ancient deities, they could never be pleased. They were always angry, and you always had to walk on eggshells around them. You never knew what side of the bed they got up on that morning.

OUR GOD IS A SMILING GOD

The Lord was basically saying, "I want My people to know on a daily basis that I'm nothing like that." Paul wrote about this in the Book of Romans, "What then shall we say to these things? If God is for us, who can be against us?" (Romans 8:31) We know from Scripture that the world, the flesh, and the devil are against us, but the idea of this verse is, "Who can be against us successfully?" No one. And our Lord wants us to live with that kind of confidence. He wants the truth of the greatness of His love for us continually reinforced in our lives. Sometimes even the strongest of us can find ourselves doubting His love or at least not being as confident of His love as we ought to be.

You might picture God looking at you with a frown of displeasure. He looks at everyone else with a big grin, but then He sees you, and His countenance changes. But the Bible says that He's a smiling God. His countenance shines when He looks at you. I would hardly believe it except it's right there in the Bible. When He looks at you and me, He smiles. That is the Father's heart toward us as His children.

Difficult times do come and go in life, but no matter how difficult a given circumstance might be, I'm all right as long as I know that He's smiling and that He's pleased with me —and He is.

Our God is a blessing God. Our God is a keeping God. *Our God is a smiling God.*

The LORD...be gracious to you....

OUR GOD IS A GRACIOUS GOD

Notice fourthly, in verse 25, that our God is a gracious God. God wants us as His people to be continually reminded that He is a gracious God and that He is a forgiving, pardoning God. He does not deal with us according to justice or what we deserve, but according to grace, on the basis of undeserved, unmerited favor.

Mercy is not getting what I do deserve; grace is getting what I don't deserve. For example, if I loaned my car to a friend to use for the day, and while driving, he became distracted and crashed my car into a tree, he owes me a new car. That's what justice demands. But if I forgave him the debt, not making him do what he deserves to do—buy me new car—that is mercy. Grace is beyond mercy. Grace would be to then take my friend out to the nicest restaurant in town for dinner, and then after dinner, go to a car lot and buy him a brand new car. The free dinner and the new car represent grace—getting what I don't deserve on top of not getting what I do deserve. That is God's nature and the way He deals with us as His children.

The fact of the matter is that every one of us is in need of God's grace on a daily basis; and every day God wants us to know that it is available.

OUR GOD IS A BLESSING GOD

Some people believe that once they are born again, they never sin again. However, the Bible says, "If we say that we have no sin, we deceive ourselves, and the truth is not in us" (1 John 1:8). Every one of us sins every single day. To sin is simply to be less than perfect, and every day each of us is less than like Jesus in action, in speech, in thought, and in motive. Sin includes not only acts of commission, doing what is wrong, but also acts of omission, knowing to do right in a situation, but failing to obey. Not one single human being can lay their head down on the pillow at the end of the day and say to God, "Lord, I would love to confess my sins to You and ask for Your forgiveness, but in every word, in every deed, in every thought, and in every motive, I was exactly like Jesus today."

Every one of us is in need of God's grace on a daily basis, and every day God wants us to know that it is available.

The fact of the matter is that every one of us falls short of His perfect standard, and thus when Jesus taught the disciples how to pray, a part of that prayer stated, "Forgive us our debts" (Matthew 6:12). We know that that prayer is a daily prayer because it includes the petition, "Give us *this day* our daily bread" (Matthew 6:11, emphasis mine). That model prayer includes a daily confession of sin and a daily request for forgiveness. Why? Because the best of us, the most highly motivated of us, sin daily, and we are daily in need of God's grace.

The Lord knows that, and He knows we need to be assured that He is a gracious, pardoning, and forgiving God. So when we sin or fall short of

Christ-likeness, first we confess our sin to Him and ask for His forgiveness. Secondly, we confess our sin to and ask forgiveness from the person we have sinned against. We then can move on in His grace. God's grace protects us from condemnation and crushing guilt — a protection each of us needs this side of Heaven.

I think it is important to recognize the difference between conviction and condemnation. God will convict me of sin, but conviction will always draw me toward God for forgiveness. Condemnation occurs when I become aware of my sin and then begin to have feelings that drive me away from God. Thoughts like, "Do you actually think you can just come back to God and receive forgiveness after what you've done? You better just lay low for a few days to let God cool off and maybe forget what you've done a little bit before you even think about praying to Him again!"

The conviction of the Holy Spirit will *always* draw me back to God and introduce hope into the situation on the basis of God's grace. Condemnation will drive me from Him in the consciousness of my own unworthiness, which means I am relating to God on the basis of my works rather than on the basis of His grace. Why would God remind His people every day that He is a gracious God? Because He knows that we are going to need grace every day, and He wants us to know that He has it for us. When we fail, we may surprise ourselves, but we never surprise the Lord. He has perfect knowledge of our frailties and need for His grace.

Maybe today is the day that you need to leave "that" sin or failure from your past in His gracious hands once and for all. That sin from last

When we fail, we may surprise ourselves, but we never surprise the Lord.

week or last year. That sin from five, ten, twenty, or fifty years ago that rises up from your past and produces deep shame, which sends you tumbling into condemnation. You have lived it over and over and over again in your mind, wishing there was some way to undo it. The Bible says that where sin abounds, grace hyper-abounds (Romans 5:20).

Picture this: you're on a beach and you've built a sandcastle, which represents your sin. You're fretting over how big it is and wondering if God has the grace to wash it away. Then, all of a sudden, you hear about an incoming tidal wave, which represents God's grace. The wave not only washes away the sandcastle, but it takes out ten miles of the California coastline. That is what Paul is saying there in Romans, where sin abounds — when it looks so big, so ugly, so permanent, and so forever — grace hyper-abounds.

There isn't any sin greater than Calvary. No sin is greater than God's grace and desire to forgive one of His children.

Commit that past sin to the Lord right now and any time during the rest of your life that it rises up in your mind and exalts itself against the knowledge of God, rises up against what you know to be true about God. Bring that thought into captivity and cry out in your heart and mind, "My God is a gracious, forgiving God. I reject that thought as unworthy of Him and unworthy of one who has been forgiven by so great a Savior on Calvary's tree." Then move on with your day, using it now to live a life that brings blessing and glory to Him. If that thought comes into your mind forty times a day, then do this forty times a day. Next week, it will only be twenty times, and the week after that, ten times, until finally it will only attempt to surface occasionally, and even then unsuccessfully, as it is met with that bold, God-honoring confidence in the fact that our God is a gracious God.

None of us will ever outgrow the need to be constantly reminded of the grace of God. Sometimes, the more mature we become in the Lord, the more important it is for us to realize how gracious He is. It seems the more we become like Christ, the more conscious we are of just how far we have yet to go. I think of the Apostle Paul in all of this. Early in his writings, he declared to the church in Corinth that he was the least of the apostles (1 Corinthians 15:9). Then he wrote to the church in Ephesus and declared that he was the least of the saints (Ephesians 3:8). When he got to the end of his life, he wrote to Timothy and declared himself the chiefest of sinners (1 Timothy 1:15). He was never more holy or Christ-like than at the end of his life, but at the same time, he was more conscious of his need for God's grace and of God's rich, abundant supply than ever.

> *The more we become like Christ, the more conscious we are of just how far we have yet to go.*

Our God is a blessing God. Our God is a keeping God. Our God is a smiling God. *Our God is a gracious God.*

The LORD lift up His countenance upon you....

OUR GOD IS AN ATTENTIVE GOD

Notice number five from verse 26. God wanted Moses to declare, "The LORD lift up His countenance upon you." That phrase, "to lift up His countenance," or "to lift up His face," literally means, "to look, to see, to know, to be interested, to have one's full attention." God is declaring, "I want My people to know that I am an attentive God."

Have you ever walked into a room where the person you love most in life is seated, and upon your entrance into the room, they put down everything in which they were previously engaged in order to give you their full and undivided attention? How does that make you feel? It really feels good, doesn't it? It makes us feel very special and very loved, and it makes us realize how blessed we are to have such a person in our lives.

The Lord wants us to know that that's what He does every time we come to Him; indeed, it is what He is toward us all the time. In essence, God is saying, "I want My people reminded every single day that they have My full and undivided attention." He's attentive to us, He's interested in us, He cares about us, He watches over us, and He always hears us.

OUR GOD IS A BLESSING GOD

There are those times that all of us experience where we wonder whether He really cares about what we're going through. "Does He even know what's going on? Is there a place I can send a cablegram or a registered letter and let Him know about the terrible circumstance I am in? For surely inattentiveness can be the only explanation for the longevity of this trial." Well, the Lord says, "I want My people to know every day that I am Emmanuel," which is interpreted, "God with us." He knows what we're going through, every bit of it, every square inch.

I want My people reminded every single day that they have My full and undivided attention.

Consider the life of Joseph (Genesis 30-50). Think about all those long years—from the time he received those glorious visions from God of future promotion and blessing, to the time he was sold into slavery, to the day he finally became the second most powerful man in the world. For years, it looked like God didn't care, as if the visions that God had given him were just a cruel tease. For years, it looked like God had forgotten him. But the fact of the matter is that God was watching and attentive every moment, attentive to every twist and turn of events. In fact, He was orchestrating all of it toward His end. The Lord knew that one day He was going to make Joseph the second most powerful man in the world. But He also knew, and He alone knew at the time, the kind of character that Joseph would need to have built into his life to properly handle the position that God had ordained for him.

OUR GOD IS AN ATTENTIVE GOD

That is one of the "problems" God faces concerning our lives. He is "a blessing God," but He also knows that He must develop our character and faith sufficiently to handle His blessings in a spiritually mature way. This will often require hard times for us when He forces us to learn to walk by faith and not by sight. It will mean times when it will seem like He has forgotten about us and that He doesn't care about us, times when we don't feel Him, times when it seems like He has gone silent. And God, knowing that there would be such times in the lives of His people, wanted them to be reminded daily of the fact that He is an attentive God. We have His undivided attention.

For years, God's dealings in the life of Joseph looked unfair and even cruel. Then everything changed in one day, and Joseph went from being a Jewish prisoner in an Egyptian prison to being the most powerful man in the world next to Pharaoh himself. Joseph and everyone else could look back and see God's fingerprints everywhere on all the events of those long years of preparation when it looked like He wasn't doing anything. No, He had been an attentive God all along. Every promise He gave to Joseph proved to be "amen and amen." The promises, however, were also coupled with the godly character needed for Joseph to safely enjoy them.

He knows what we're going through, every bit of it, every square inch.

Our God is a blessing God. Our God is a keeping God. Our God is a smiling God. Our God is a gracious God. *Our God is an attentive God.*

The LORD...give you peace.

OUR GOD IS A PEACE-GIVING GOD

Lastly, He declares, "...and give you peace." The Lord wants us to know that He is a peace-giving God. I don't know how many of you have been to Israel before, but one of the first words you learn upon arrival is shalom. That's the word used for peace here in this verse — shalom.

The Jews, when they greet one another or say good-bye to one another, say, "shalom." And when the Jews say hello and good-bye by saying shalom, they're not just saying hello and good-bye, they are actually pronouncing a blessing over that person. They are pronouncing peace upon them, not just the absence of conflict or the absence of war in their life, but a prayer for the general well-being of the person. It's similar to our "God bless you." I say, "God bless you" a lot to people, especially when we are saying good-bye. It is not mere Christian-eze or vain repetition to me, it is a prayer asking for God's blessing upon their lives. It is the desire for God's best in their lives. In the same sense, shalom to the Jews is a prayer over a person's life. To declare shalom to someone is to want the very best for them in life.

In the same way, the Lord wants us to be reminded daily of the fact that He desires the very best for our lives. Every day when they heard,

"...and give you peace," it was a needed, daily reminder that their God only wanted the very best for them.

The Lord also wants us to know that when He says, "...and give you peace," or shalom, it is a reminder that He desires the best for our lives. God knows that there is a relationship between my knowing He only wants the very best and my experiencing the presence of peace in my life. For God knows that when we really and truly understand that He only wants what is best for us in our lives, that realization will translate into a life of peace and rest.

God answers all my prayers the same way I would answer them if I had His wisdom, power, and love.

Years ago someone wrote, "God nothing doest nor suffers to be done but what thou wouldest thyself do couldest thou see the end of all He does as well as He." I have a friend who has walked with the Lord for almost seventy years who took that saying and restated it this way, "God answers all my prayers the same way I would answer them if I had His wisdom, power, and love." I think that's so outstanding! Let's read it again, "God answers all my prayers the same way I would answer them if I had His wisdom, power, and love." If we only knew how concerned and how active He is for our well-being and for the very best in our lives, we would rest much more than we do. We would have much more peace than we do. Our God is a peace-giving God; He only wants the best for us. To know that truth is to enter into rest.

OUR GOD IS A PEACE-GIVING GOD

So they shall put My name on the children of Israel....

In verse 27, God declared to Moses, "So they shall put My name on the children of Israel...." In the United States' culture, a name is for the most part simply a means of identification, a way to differentiate myself from the rest of humanity, allowing you to call my name from across a crowded room and get my attention. In the Hebrew culture, the name of a person represented much more than that. A name represented the character and nature of the person. And here the Lord is declaring that this blessing is more than just a blessing—it's a representation of His nature. He is saying in essence, "This is exactly who I am and what I am to My people, not occasionally, not on special days, this is who I am and what I am all the time. Moses, have this pronounced over My people again and again, even every day, to remind them because I know how easily they forget."

Our God is a blessing God. Our God is a keeping God. Our God is a smiling God. Our God is a gracious God. Our God is an attentive God. *Our God is a peace-giving God.*

...I will bless them.

OUR GOD KEEPS HIS PROMISES

Finally, notice what is perhaps the most astonishing thing of all about the entire passage in verse 27, when the Lord says, "and I will bless them." I love that, "I will." Translation? "You who have spiritual oversight of My people, pronounce this blessing in all of its strength, and I WILL LIVE UP TO EVERY BIT OF IT IN THEIR LIVES. Don't make excuses for Me; don't hedge on any of it. Don't soft sell it or explain it away. Don't be afraid that they're going to put expectations upon Me that I'm not going to be able to fulfill. Do some sanctified boasting in Me. Tell them in every single spiritual meeting that has anything to do with Me that this is who and what I am, and I will be faithful to live up to every bit of it in their lives." Astonishing!

And so He has, and so He will.

So, what is our God really like?

Our God is a blessing God.

Our God is a keeping God.

Our God is a smiling God.

OUR GOD IS A BLESSING GOD

Our God is a gracious God.

Our God is an attentive God.

Our God is a peace-giving God.

Six truths that He wants us to be continually reassured of as we make our way toward our heavenly Home. *This* is who He is and what He is like. This is what He will be faithful to be every single day of our pilgrimage. Praise the Lord!

INVITATION

Perhaps you have read this book, but you yourself don't have a personal relationship with God. Everything that He has described Himself to be, He desires to be personally in your life. Beginning that personal relationship with Him is very simple.

1) The Bible teaches us that God loves us and wants to have a personal relationship with us.

    God is love.

    > 1 John 4:8, emphasis mine

    But God demonstrates His own love toward us, in that while we were still sinners, Christ died for us.

    > Romans 5:8, emphasis mine

2) The "bad news" is that our sin has separated us from God and the relationship for which we were created.

    For *all have sinned and fall short* of the glory of God....

    > Romans 3:23, emphasis mine

3) But the "good news" is that God loved us so much that He sent His Son Jesus to pay the price we couldn't pay for the forgiveness of our sins.

OUR GOD IS A BLESSING GOD

For God so loved the world that He gave His only begotten Son, that whoever believes in Him should not perish but have everlasting life.

John 3:16-17, emphasis mine

4) I personally receive God's forgiveness and salvation by turning from my old sinful ways, trusting in Jesus' death upon the cross as the satisfying payment for the forgiveness of my sins, and surrendering my life to God to be used for His purposes. When you do this, God's Holy Spirit personally comes into your heart and begins to develop the character of Jesus *within* you and to live the life of Jesus *through* you. Jesus' life was the most attractive and blessed life ever lived on this earth. To enter into this relationship is to enter into life as God intends it for you. It is truly the greatest life imaginable.

If you would like to begin this personal relationship with God, you can do so right now by sincerely praying...

"Dear Lord Jesus, I confess that I am a sinner and that I have been less than perfect in my life. Thank You for dying on the cross for my sins. Right now, I turn from my old sinful ways, and I surrender my life to You. Please take control of it and make me into the person You want me to be. Thank You for forgiving my sins and giving me everlasting life. Amen."

INVITATION

If you prayed that prayer, you have now begun a personal relationship with the God who has been described in this book! Next, you need to take some practical steps to grow strong spiritually: read the Bible, pray, and go to a Bible-teaching church to learn more about what it means to be a Christian. The Lord bless you and keep you! He promises He will.

OTHER BOOKS BY DAMIAN KYLE

The Place of Brokenness in the Life of the Believer

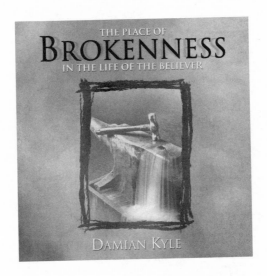

ISBN: 1931667527

OTHER MATERIALS AVAILABLE

Visit Calvary Chapel Modesto's website for additional audio messages by Pastor Damian Kyle. Access them by logging onto their website at:

http://www.calvarychapelmodesto.com

Audio tapes are also available by calling 209-545-5530, by writing to 4300 American Avenue, Modesto, California 95356, or by e-mailing tapelibrary@ calvarychapelmodesto.com.